EATING THE STING

EATING
THE
STING

including

The

Heronry

by

John Caddy

MILKWEED EDITIONS

89 88 87 86   4 3 2 1

A LAKES & PRAIRIES AWARD BOOK
Published by *Milkweed Editions*
Post Office Box 3226
Traffic Station
Minneapolis, Minnesota 55403
Books may be ordered from the above address

Designed and illuminated by R.W. Scholes ©1986
Edited by Emilie Buchwald

Library of Congress Cataloging-in-Publication Data

Caddy, John
  EATING THE STING

  A Lakes and Prairies Award Book

  I. Title.
PS3553.A313E28 1986   811'.54   86-62393
ISBN 0-915943-19-0

This publication is supported in part by a grant provided
by the Metropolitan Regional Arts Council from funds
appropriated by the Minnesota State Legislature.

for Lin,
who makes it possible

FOREWORD

The title poem of *Eating the Sting* is about transforming pain into song, and the title is descriptive of the whole book. Caddy speaks in one poem of children "astonished that humans could be numb." Before pain can be made into song, it must be felt, and Caddy's poems strive to bring us out of the anaesthesia of civilized life.

To call John Caddy's poems "nature poems" is a little like calling Bob Dylan "a musician." It's true, but it misses the point. Probably nobody else has written about nature the way Caddy has. Thoreau is closest, but Caddy is concerned with feeling as Thoreau was not. Caddy shares Thoreau's way of meeting nature and finding lessons that are not obvious. Like Thoreau chasing the woodchuck, Caddy gives us civilization relearning wildness by breaking free of observational custom.

In "The Heronry" (which could fairly be called a novella cast in songs and tales and prose poems), we are immersed in the double consciousness of a girl and a disembodied natural historian. At its conclusion, there is no distinction between the mysteries of nature and the mysteries of humanity, and neither is quite so mysterious as it had been, mystery having been transformed into memory via experience.

Eating the Sting is a chronicle of *encounters* with nature — wilderness carefully blundered into, predators adapted to city life, whales revivified by imagination in the dark. But Caddy has no nature nostalgia, no inclination to settle for pop sublimity. His encounters are as likely to be with voles and fledgling kingfishers and stray dogs as with bears and hawks.

Caddy's language, like a stretch of forest, is dense and multitextured, and demands attention to unexpected detail. Sometimes, odd compound words spring up like weeds splitting rock — or like the cry of an animal laying open our own animal insides. "We cannot name this cry," Caddy tells us, in a poem in which he names it in a dozen ways. This book is full of names discovered and preserved. This is a book full of names. To seek language is to discover nature, and to discover ourselves. We cast off anaesthesia by the pain and joy of naming. Our nature is to feel and speak. *Eating the Sting* presents a natural history of ex-Europeans seeking a North American ecological niche.

John Rezmerski

The author wishes to thank Jerome Bach, Carrol Henderson, Rodger Kemp and George Roberts for reading the text, answering bird questions, tolerating odd-hour phone calls to hear poems, and generally attending this book's birth.

Some of these poems have previously appeared, in earlier form, in the following publications: *Beloit Poetry Journal, Dacotah Territory, Great River Review* and *Milkweed Chronicle.*

CONTENTS

EATING THE STING

BOTTOMLAND

HEALING THE VOICE

THE HERONRY

EATING THE STING

EATING THE STING

Caught in the snapped circle of light
on the cookshack oilcloth,
an upright deermouse holding yellow
in her fine fingers
like an ear of black-striped corn,
a wasp I'd slapped dead earlier.

She stares, belly resonating, round above
a scatter of brittle wing, bits, a carapace —
she has already eaten the stinger —
stares at me, still,
something thrumming in her eyes

beyond herself, a mouse stung
onto an edge as far from cartoons
as the venom she's chewed into food.

She cocks a fawn ear now, trembling poisonchanger,
caught in the circle of light
I've thought myself in at times,

but never sure, I ask her softly how
she does it, if I can learn this turning
of sting into such food as startles in her eyes,
learn to suck pain into every sense
and come up spitting seeds, force poison
to a tear held fierce between my lips
and whirl it into tongue which sings, but

here I've come too loud: She drops the husk,
fusses whiskers with her paws, kicks
a scrap of wing aside, and whispers
thanks for the corn,

steps backward off the table
(and so potent she is with wasp)
flips a circle through light and
lands running on her leaf-toed feet.

FISHER LOON

a ritual for ridding

The still glacial lake, our canoe
wake bowstrung through sunrise
mist burning off black rocks
thrust sudden out of white:

What is driftwood resolves into
a coarse circle of sticks and stems
under two large eggs speckled
brown on olive, around them slung

the long smooth body of the loon,
flattened in the hollow of the nest
black and white, watching us
her wet eye — she snakes up,

drops off the rockshelf beating
lake into wingwater cast into sun,
stands on her tail,
opens her voice and casts for us,

sinks it back deep in our throats
(bright tears in laughter loon caught)
drags one wing half unfurled, tip
breaking the surface ripple, mother

cripple setting the hook, sculls back
to the canoe, opens her voice and
glories us away (and what can we do
but follow) until

far enough: the siren laughs, beats
her wings whole, shakes sleek
and quietly dives.

Eating the Sting

THE COURTSHIP OF THE WOODCOCK

Near dusk, the western sun outlining gravel ruts.
All afternoon he grubbed earthworms from the mud.

Later his wings will make song — no metaphor — real wind
through real feathers the colors of netted leaves,
astonishing warbles and whistles.

In the climax of his courtship, in twilight or the moon,
he will climb a helix written in the air for him, spiral
thirty feet straight up, wings trilling, circle
at the top and plummet openbeaked to ground,

a pattern welded to each coiled spring unwinding
in his genes, as this spring uncoils from winter
snow persistent under spruces, but now

near dusk on one of those back roads which lead us
to the wearing of a guise we take on unaware,

we meet him in the humming of the circle's finding,
not its piercing, where the river tongues the bank,
where the wave persuades the shore, as he walks
the ritual near puddles in the gravel road.

Somewhere close the female crouches, secret in weeds.
We are all most lovely not making love but just before.

The woodcock struts the road behind his downcurved beak,
the neckless featherbody ball perched on stilts,
pure seducer sparkling in his eye,

dropping one foot down from one long backhinged leg,
his body sinking on it to the ground and rising,
then the other stilt unfolds and drops and body follows it,

and up, the cadenced settling into ground and rising slow,
the rhythm of the wave upon the shore we catch in that suspended
moment when we in courtship first read in coupled eyes
that we will make love,

so the woodcock's urgent untimed ritual floats above gravel,
master, the held line of his body and long beak absolute.

When he stops our breaths go on with him, the whole
swelling landscape moves on with him: weeds, the puddled road,
the alders, spruce, the falling sun our bodies all
lifting and dropping while the woodcock holds the center,

the power, this pure possession of spring.

Eating the Sting

BEARWAKING

I walk tangled in sun,
and the redwings dance willow buds
into gut-sung green.
Catkins drift into muskeg.

And swinging a stick
down an old logging trail,
round a hazelbrush turn
and there *Jesus a bear!* muzzle up
(slack-sided, fresh from the sleep)
eyes lock a long beat — he

wheels and claws flash white
from the shoulder roll gait
and I stand struck:

Drop my ear to the ground,
strain the pawbeats of that bulk
through the heart-hammered ear.

Roll over: a marsh hawk banks,
small birds skitter the brush again,
balm of gilead musk, a spider silk shines,
all the small graces tang.

I lie budded in roots.
There is pollen in my beard.
(His print begins to gleam with wet.)

EYE OF TOAD

The mouth is wide, habit of hunger,
stretched drum throat trembles, alive, and
the fourth finger quivers in its sleep.

Eyes of wet gold netted in sable,
intuitive lessons in dream.
(Cellini cried when he saw these eyes.)

In greens and blues a fly shines and preens.
A white nerve throbs between hunger and gold,
quickens the throat to tongue–

–song!   A wing spirals in jarred light.
The eyes swallow closed, content,
and slow as their depth arise and gaze again

in dreams of gold and sanguine consummations, and
the fourth finger quivers in its sleep.

BEYOND SILENCE

Swinging open our arms,
beating them back
loud in the cold air,
we stared at the lake,
whitecapped and black, rolling
as our father evoked
flights of mallards
scudding like low clouds
over the blind.

Lake Winnibigoshish,
the slow browns of fall,
ducksback coat stiff on my shoulders
as I swung my arms.

Away from the shore, in dry ferns
I found on its back a whole
turtle shell and skeleton.
The legs were perfect, each
white bone intact and thinly held,
the links of the tail,
his skull, jaw slightly open,
neckbones curving back into the hollow shell.

I saw him green.

In the wind it was
so still. Saw
him green, tipped somehow
on his back,
waving his corded legs for days.
Mouth windsucking, neck
bow-arched against the ground,
always four legs straining
for purchase, the granite outcrop
beyond his reach but seen,
voiceless and waving.

When I touched him the legs and head
shivered and fell, the thin bones
mixing in lichens, leaving the unmoved shell.

ENCOUNTER WITH A COOPER'S HAWK
a ritual for seeing

Hawk,
fifteen times
you hurtled toward my eyes,
swept first the hat,
then the hair,
when finally my refusals
failed your patience,
and you sang talons
through my tightened scalp.

Over and over
you screamed
and launched yourself
from a cedar bough
while I stood scared
and rooted in my need.

Forgive me,
in the name of your nest,
in the name of your mate
shrieking from a near tree,
for using you to practice open eyes.

Over and over
you flung into my face
telescoped
black talons, black
beaktips, the clarity
and test of adamant sight,

and still in sleep,
you soar from wounded mystery,
a sudden shadow made of light,
and scatter on my night the shapes of wings.

Eating the Sting

SHARING THE CRY
for Owen

We cannot name this sound.   It locks the jaw.
It curls the tongue into the shapes
of sucking marrow from the bone.

From the pines a scream across the lake,
at first a woman's scream—but more, no hint of fear,
an endless wailing high and sliding down at last
to break on teeth and tongue, a celebration
of the lungs, a chilling song from somewhere
wet and warm, with overtones of spit and fur.

It shocks the muscles cramped,
leaves hands clamped tight around the paddle's shaft
and leaves the ear dazzled like the eye
by splintered waves reflecting light.

We cannot name this cry, but know
that this was animal, raw, entire,
and through the leaping drum of heart and ear,
the texture on our skins of standing fur,
we slowly realize that this was cougar's scream.

After, we hear no sound, make none.
Our faces pale, scanning trees, we watch
a heron lumber out of reeds, getting out of there.
We drift in the canoe and try to breathe.
We smile, and know one meaning of *alive.*

There are no cougars left up here, they say.
Does echo drain the marrow from the bone?
We know what's real: this cry
which strains our jaws to silence, and echoes
in our hollowing an old taut-sinewed fear
from the open throat of time.   Without this cry
which curls the tongue into such shapes as these,
we are shrunken.   With it, we are more.

QUESTIONS FOR THE KINGFISHER

The primary cause of mortality
in fledgling kingfishers is
drowning while learning to fish

1 First Things First

there's grey in your blue,
old spear-billed fisher king

blue from sunlight and for sky

grey from flight in all dimensions
of transparency

he clatters wet blue feathers into light,
shakes his raggedy crest
and flies to eat

you who for every meal must
try this water gasp
and break twice the swaying mirror

are you fooled too
in your reflections?

he clatters wet blue feathers into light,
shakes his crest
and flies to eat

Eating the Sting

2 *Sharing Essence*

both big-headed,
eccentric in flight, crochety
voices rattling on, and
for a crest of tattered feathers
a foolscap crown, but

you move fluently
through everything that rings
clear as water, clear as air

you eat and teach
the children of the nest
by spearing through clear water

can poets flow through
that hard clarity they seek
though fledglings sometimes drown?

3 Evolving

fish and fisherbird
silver and greyblue

shaped by flowing
through clear simples

ova, water, air

once-shaped silver fish
twice-shaped fisherbird

greyblue

do poems take their shapes
and breathe their songs
through drowning's thickened air?

4 *Fisher in That Fine Suspension*

like the clear moment
when the poet
forces gutsong into voice

the endless trembling hover
then the plunge

to what flashes silver
in suddenly
transparent depths

to drop into such
painful clarity
that he may drown

then
water shatter, sky

like an old poet
rising from an image into air

shakes the draggled feathers
shakes the ragged crown
and flies rattling off
to shape quick silver
into bone

THE YAWN

If you are hearing this poem, try not to yawn.
We are wholly inside ourselves
when we're inside a yawn.
I want you to hear this. Don't yawn.
But do try the word: drop the jaw and know
the vowel lying in the bottom of your mouth.
Yawn. Go ahead, say it: Yawn.
But don't do it. Don't even think
about doing it. Do not recall the inward
pleasure of this stretching of the jaws.
Above all, don't imagine how yawns start:
the sensation at the back of the jaw,
the beginning tightness of the throat,
its echo that begins below your tongue and
tightens, and like a loose but heavy spring
pulls your jaw down, and further down until
your cheeks stretch and you gasp air in,
tongue clamped to the mouthfloor and pushing hard,
and stretching incredibly more, hear the small
roaring in your ears and holding the stretch,
holding until release, the jaw shuddering up
like a child's trying to speak through tears,
the quaver of the neck and skull—

Such meanings we attach to mouths,
and the endless words they make.
Go back. Go back to speechless
tongues to find our root
connections to skin and fur and scale.

Everything with jaws knows how to yawn, and must.
There is a joining of all lives with jaws:
unwilled, we lick, we touch, we hunger, and we yawn.

Infants yawn before they're born, and we
are infants when we yawn, half our eyes are closed.
All creatures then without defense, all
returning to beginnings, all flowing down the trunk
to roots, returning to the egg or womb.

When we see a squirrel yawn, arrested
halfway up a tree, or a tortoise stretching out
his leather beak, or watch a small child
in pajamas, holding one fist over it, denying
he is tired, or a puppy's stumbling yawn
as he curls himself to sleep,

When we see a toad's wide mouth do this
after swallowing a bug, or a girl in lamplight
yawning, putting down her book, or taken unawares,
a snake's delicious gaping in the sun,

We must show our yawns to them, and through them
smile, and know a tenderness, a kinship there:
we are wholly inside them, as if
they were all our children, all
our wards, the ones we must protect.

WHY GRANDFATHERS ARE GENTLER
THAN THEIR SONS

As I hunker in a march meadow, touching in dead grass
the fugitive shapes of mouse tunnels once lively under snow,
my hand traces the bones of a milkweed to the pods,
and something thaws through my fingertips, a knowing
about milkweed pods and the sadness of men:

That from the softness of our first green swelling
              we twist and harden on the stem,

That we learn to wear these grey rough husks,
              this hairy warty hide,

That we can open, in any season, any fierceness of wind,

That the rich white milk we suck from earth
              we cast floating into sky
                   to find dark earth again,

That inside we carry a skin so smooth it catches breath,
              a mirror of the warm skin
                  high on woman's inner thigh,

That this birth-echo skin, once thrown open,
              survives the cold as well as any rugged hide,

That many do not know until their seeds are spent and grown
              that their cracked husks own an inside,

That some never open, and hang clutched into themselves
              fighting imaginary knives of winter wind,

That a milkweed pod in its completion is neither empty
              nor hollow, but simply open
                  in the sun.

Eating the Sting

OLD BACHELOR OFFERINGS

He rises from the slough like history,
cattails sluicing from his shell.
The huge snapper rises breathing, bubbles on the nostrils,
gusty breaths blessing lungs
empty all the icelocked darkness,
since ice first sang thinly in November wind,
and thickened, and locked him in.
Sluggish he comes from the silence of waiting,
where the year slowly rotted
and sifted down to coat his shell,
where he lay dim for months like an ancient stone.

But this is waking: now
he pushes clumps of ice aside, black honeycombs
dissolving into sun and muskrats' paddling,
now he staggers through sedgemat and mud
dragging long algae streamers.
He is cloaked with leeches, festooned with black
twisting, recoiling from sudden brightness and heat.
He stops and gusts air, snorkel nose straining high.
In a straight line he flounders on, crushing cattails under him.

Weedslap: jerks his head in, stops.   Rotates his eyes.
Old man gumming his jaws, he works his beak from side to side,
cautions his head out, and shoves his way up the gravel bank,
liftng his bulk step by step and sliding back, clawing up again
all pitted plates and scales the color of drying algae
beneath the frantic, tiring leeches.   He breaks the crest
and gasping sprawls, clusters of snails huddled
in loose folds of skin

> like an old bachelor lumberjack
> in baggy longjohns winterstained
> all the colors of a deeryard thaw,
> who buttonless had sewn himself into them
> last November, logged in them,
> cooked in them, spilled on them,
> slept the long incontinent darknesses in them
> until they were both a season's record
> and a second skin.

He sags at an oilclothed table next to a stove,
one bony hand resting in a net of sunlight,
chapped pores open to this heat.
His hand knows it is almost May
and time to shed the winter skin,
time to bare himself to sun
that winter burn from him.
The fingers curl and drum.

A flap of longjohns!
and he's leaping out the door
to purge himself in sunlight
on the matted grass,
He whirls barefoot among stumps
in the madness of Spring,
reeling at his chest
but he can't find the threads,
finds a rent and rips it wide,
shucks them to his ankles,
hopping in gaunt arabesques.
Like a boy he hurls up his arms,
stretching blue shadowed ribs,
and offers his paleness to the sun.
But his lungs cannot catch
this trembling air, he weaves
exhausted spirals toward a center
where he sinks

so the old bachelor drags himself,
abrading his sunken plastron with winter debris.
He knows this hurts, he knows this is laborious,
he knows his stomach is a shriveled kernel in his gut,
but he knows the sun is here and he has to get the damned things off.
He lumbers into light, crushing last year under him.

He scrapes and burns the winter from his shell and skin,
a trail of leeches, snails and algae threads dropping
as he ploughs another hundred yards.
On a mat of snow-flattened grass he stops to bask,

ragged legs outstretched, tendons in his neck
stretching the sun as it weaves from side to side.
With a hind foot he shoves himself in a slow revolution,
catching brilliance in the darkest pockets of his skin.

Enough.   He takes his bearings
and lurches back along his path.   Stops.   Notices.
What are these black dying questions curled in wintered grass?
He noses one, snaps and gulps, and pushes off toward the slough.
He has made his offering.
They were Winter. Who thinks in Spring?

SPRING SWAMP, FULL MOON

In the night, in the ponds
I walk thigh wet,

A season's deaths layer the mud
pulling me in,

Frogs hang from moonlight
by their eyes,

shrilling of months stunned
alive, alone,

Cattails angle white in dark water,
flatworms on a dying blade—

Mouths, all the searching
soft mouths

pulling me in, a small and cold but
singing thing,

Bubbles of swamp gas laze to the moon
as I wobble and lurch,

From fall's brown scuttle,
tendrils of algae green.

Frogs are not mad.
The comfort in mud isn't cold.

RITUAL FOR HAIRWASHING
Manitou River, Lake Superior

The woman sits in her skin
on riverwet stone, leaned
back on a split slab of rock,
warming in the early light.
Her legs are spread to morning,
cut off at the calves in a boiling
mirror which breaks into foam
as it touches her skin, red
to the knees, everywhere else
loose with sun.

From wrists she thrusts forward,
flings over her face her long black hair,
and draws an arch with her spine
from river to stone.
Stares down at fragments of her face
dancing in the shadows of her hair.
Plunges her head into the cold
pressure of the mirror and lifts
gasping, she gathers and soaps her hair,
slips off the stone and flows
into the darkness under the mirror.

Leaps up from rinsing goosebumped and taut,
hands to hipbones, elbows akimbo,
and circling from the waist,
whirls that darkness in a gleaming hoop,
whirls it wet into comets and sparks,
voicing it now,
sound rises wordless
from her belly to her teeth,
and balanced on stones
she casts shouts in a ring to the sky
to fuse the river and sun.

Slows, breathing gusts.
Head bowed, her hair
sways across water.

She stands wholly defined
watching skeins of hair
drop light back into the mirror.
Shivers.   Bright neckbones
pluck the wet skin.

.

THE SALT CRIES REMEMBER

The foetus yawns in the sea,
adrift in the cell memories.

We are the sea in a skin,
the craving of salt for the ocean.

We batter the wet from our flesh,
but the land we hunched onto is dry.

What is salt is the sweet
bitter gift of the tidepool.

The tonguetip, helpless, remembers.
The sea knows itself in our juices.

We answer rain with our tears,
answer love with our drifting, our cries.

SALTFLOWERS

At first flowers, orange
tossing
over past the mint
and rhubarb gone to seedstalk,

the outhouse a tangle
of weathered boards
sinking, holes
porcupine chewed.

Orange wildflowers — strike
flowers — *butterflies*,
monarchs, so many
leafing up
as I bruise through the mint,

a weaving tapestry
clustered and fanning
in a wandering hole
so I hunker,

sweep a hand over, wings
fan my wrist, enough
lift and swirl that I see
they swarm a saltlick,
deep one,

deer tongued from sandy loam,
a shape licked smooth
and undulant, muscled out
as whitewater carves creekstone.

The swirl settles,
orange on black,
spiral tongues uncoiling
into shadewet to dab
and dab for salt.

My tongue stabs the cheek
and wonders:

The craving.

Them too.

ISHMAEL IN THE WHITE AGAIN

As snowgrains sift quietly from grey
overcast which sinks into the ghosts of spruce
across the white marsh,

As sap turns ice inside the birch and splits
the trunk and the muffled shot lifts nothing
from trees or drifts,

the only other sound the creak of boots on snow,
As nostrils slam white with cold each breath,
something above me answers it,

A great voice chuckles loud and twice,
a laugh dark as a dream's hot rag of night
answers all of it — there,

The raven, huddled guttural and huge
on the top bone of a tamarack, swings her beak
above a shaggy throat,

This black and stubborn heat inside the north
who knows tomorrow or tomorrow will bring tracks,
and flesh enough at the end of them,

Who croaks and chuckles and steams:
Rejoice! A furnace is the heart, and red!
Who gives a damn for white?

EATING THE STING

41

FOR FORGETTING

Sung awake by whales keening through
a Minnesota January night, clear
minors, massive groaning harmonies.

I lie in gooseflesh thinking it out,
discounting this or that, shiver and hunch
to the thermometer plunging and know

that in the railroad yards,
acres of frozen tracks are contracting
and beginning to sing this high elongate
wailing so like the songs of humpbacked whales.

All night I work to forget what I know,
and my ears do find whales, but at four the shuddering
clang of braking boxcars betrays me.

•

In the brightbitten morning I hear a spring
sacrament, the whitethroated sparrow
singing, and for three dawns after,
pure meee, pure meee, pure mystery,
its thin white lilting no mistake.

But in the smoking firstlight my eye
tracks the song to the oak and the mimic bluejay
who has saved up this song, but discovered,
breaks off to render his own cackle and scold,

for truth has fled south, and in this iron north,
the whitethroated sparrow is sung by the jay.

•

I have always loved the impure,
and if whalesongs can leap a continent of ice
to translate railroad yards into the sea,
and the whitethroat be sung by the jay,
I will not daze my ear with my brain.

These winters breed us for forgetting.
It will not be hard, truth clangs too cold,

and thrown into winter's teeth,
all that matters is this singing.

TAIGA SNOWSHOEING

Still morning, spruce thick with new snow.
Breath is my only sound.
The first tracks I see are of voles,
delicate trails appearing
from tunnels under the snow, faint lines
of tails between bird prints,
brief journeys into night
which run five or six feet
and dive back into holes.
One visibly ends, a white thrash
within parentheses, the mark of the owl.
It is cold. The day is silent as feathers.

Suddenly between my snowshoes a partridge
explodes from deep snow,
loud drumming of wing,
powder thrown into sunlight—
I almost fall down, then she's gone,
crystals sifting over me.
A moment after, the only sign
a soft unshadowed hollow
where she sat out the storm,
and on each side,
the marks of her wing tips in snow.

Sky greying down.
Thirty below and hanging.
Two sounds: breath tinkling in ice dust,
and somewhere close
the raven scrapes her throat.

BOTTOMLAND

BOTTOMLAND

In a sullen backwater
of the bottomland,
black sawed-off pilings
curve out on the water in a long sweep
and abruptly stop.
Debris from the flood
clots the slow surface,
turning in yellow scum
broken by patches of oil.

I see a dead carp, its up eye
picked out, leaving only
the white socket.
The carp gently
lips the wet side of the near piling,
mouthing brown flood leavings, moss
and rotting wood.

A pair of rubber gloves
soaked black with oil
lie on the coarse top of the piling,
lined up as though wrists jutted from them,
both on their backs, with the fingers
full and curled as if filled with drowned flesh,
distended fingers and thumbs
gesturing, palms up.

Where I am standing the wind twitches me
the smell of the carp, of the yellow algae,
of the clots slowly turning.
The hairs rise on my arms.
I take part in these
dumb supplicating hands,
and below them,
the blind carp, mouthing.

DEFINING 'STRAY'
after the Minnesota Folk Festival

In the deep heart research labs
cleanup workers
are pulling anonymous gristle
off the ends of plastic tubes,
replacing stainless instruments in racks,
rinsing clots of blood from nylon valves.
Cutting off the nutrient
to discard separated hearts.
Scraps of tissue swirl down sinks.

Lining ceramic corridors, cages and cages
of abject dogs who've had their barks
surgically excised
grunt an unvoiced *uh-uh-uh-uh*
without aspiration,
as they are battered to the cage backs
in the evening hosing down.
Cages of soaked meowless cats
crouch and spit and relentlessly evaluate.

The chorus from the barkless labs
climbs three stories of ventilator shafts
to clever exits, each a lamp
to light the way of feet through the hospital court.

Gingham-swirling sandals and polished
cowboy boots, cuffs and soles with
no faintest scent of livestock, no dried straw.
Some carry instruments: banjos, fiddles and guitars.
Faded red bandanas twice run through the laundromat
with just a touch of bleach,

And sprinkled among calico and jeans,
T-shirts blazoned H.O.W.L.
(Help Our Wolves Live)
with a silhouetted wolf
pantomiming howls to a moon painted black,
managing only *uh-uh-uh-uh*.

They hurry to be down-home in Mayo Hall,
where they'll clap hands and sing
from mouths that never got their growth
from biting stems of grass — oh
they'll stomp and string the oldtime songs
to drown in separated hearts
what rises up
three stories from the buried labs
in barkless grunts and hisses.

ICONS OF THE HUNTERS

The field edge of harvest,
left soybeans, a thin fence row.

A dry bull thistle,
seven feet of twisted thorns
and dry seed crowns,
gaunt juiceless king
in some medieval rite,
corn ears at his feet.

The chug of shotguns,
flat, fall wind against a wire
hangs a pole to trembling.

The west sun leans into
a bright cock pheasant's
severed head on black soil,
a fresh gopher mound.
From his beak the tongue curves.

At the drainage creek,
dry corn leaves whitened
in the muskrat's tooth,
urging the veins to curl
out of this.

THE SHOTS FOCUS AND MERGE

Below old Fort Snelling, shots
quick and blending to continuous slaps
echo the flooded valley where
the Minnesota and the Mississippi roil.

A clot of men with rifles strolls along
the cinder banks of the railroad right-of-way,
firing at what moves into the flood as they approach.
They are all named LeRoy.

Basking muskrats wake to water,
their furious bodies jerking
as the shots focus and merge.

A deputy sheriff stands on the cliff
above the flood, dark and tiny from below.
His name is LeRoy.

The men volley and swig beer, shooting coon,
skunk, beercan, fox, a deer, plastic
jug, even garter snake, whatever
is displaced by the flood.

Dead fur rolls in eyespots of blood
churning into yellow.
The river grows heavier downstream.

All the gentle surrogates, all the spilled
marrow of what we displace.
The deputy's gun hears the crack and pop
and loosens in its holster.

Something red: the shots converge.
Shorebirds fly from the reloading shadows
sinking across the water.
Uprooted trees hang by their hair.

A Pontiac full of LeRoys cruises Franklin Avenue
for Indian nook that isn't pregnant.
Treatying with the white-eyes.

Between innings, the commercial:
A six-pack on a silver tray
offered by a miniskirted squaw,
the background Minnehaha Falls,
for TV, for LeRoy.

The shots focus and merge.
The river grows heavier downstream.

THAT HUMANS COULD BE NUMB

At first through the startle I worried
that something wasn't right, that
needles through skin should hurt,
that something was wrong with my hands.

For days I displayed safety pins
dangling from my palms.   I recall
a bunch of us in school, sitting at our desks
obsessed with this piercing, and at recess
scaring the little kids with our metal stigmata.

We were astonished that humans could be numb.
Witlings and naive we were, equally amazed
at oleo and TNT, nylon, TV, titanium jets,
foilwrap, tunnels, rockets and bug bombs,

So we pinched up the green earthskin
from which we sprang, and stuck pins into it
over and over, goaded the planet
cleverly, idly as kids in school,
and didn't think it hurt,

As if in our making, some connection, some
essential nerve was never quite hooked up,
or fired so slowly that we
climbed decades between wounding and pain.
Something is wrong with our hands.

THE POST-LITERATE WORLD

at the Minnesota Zoo

Just after the nocturnal exhibits
I come blinking and astonished upon 'Tapir'
with an erection longer than his legs,
and hanging on the fence three punk leathergirls
in neon hair and safety pins, giggling
at his enormous member which doesn't drag
but points ahead at thirty degrees,
and as he paces forward the tip
furrows the hoof-battered soil of his enclosure,
but the tapir doesn't wince, just
paces forward looking sidelong at the girls.

I quickly move on, completing the circle of cages,
and find still hanging there a half hour later
the same punk girls, the same captive erection
scraping foward in an interweaving pattern
of circles made of shallow grooves,
under the girls' stare like some grotesque gigolo,
eye rolling in rut, parading stupidly erect
like an obsessive night fantasy.

The foreskin is reddened and must be sore,
yet he continues pacing forward, in his own
dull tapir way the quintessential New World male
who can only seed the furrow if it causes pain.
But these trapped punk girls, my dumb embarrassment,

all this is far beyond 'Tapir,' who is simply
another caged humiliated thing
with nothing to spend his energies on,
the soil we live on too hard for furrowing,
too hard to expect much from our seed,
and all that is astonishing is that we continue
pacing forward, pretending the circles are not there.

OUTRUNNING THE THUNDERSTORM

The pickup washboards down gravel
chased by the night and storm,
the quick heat before.

A fox legs it light across the road,
spins in the lenses of headlights,
lowers his brush, slinks into weeds.

Rattles and dust, fat first drops
streaking the windshield.

A horned owl at road's edge
funnels us into his eyes,
spits us out, doesn't budge.

Thinned in our sweat we drive
always away.

Strobing over and over, beer cans
like one-eyed raccoons
thrown hot to the shoulder,
shoot our eyes back at us.

TRAPLINE

The Memory

In a mackinaw I walk as winter last light angles into the twisted roots of the cedar swamp. Hands in choppers thrust into pockets. Buckskinned hand clasps a Mason jar of overripe chickenguts. I clap my hands for warmth — the sound startles the forest, but no birds move. Underground, a snowshoe hare freezes, nose twitching. A vole running surely in a dark tunnel stops. Walking the trapline after school, checking each set. Emptying, rebaiting, resetting. Sprinkling weasel piss to mask my smell. Picking up stiff bodies, legs distorted in a last frenzy. Eyes open and filmed, staring, like tiny cold marbles when touched with an exposed finger. Tufts of frozen saliva in fur surround the leg where the jaws bit and held. Frozen arrows protecting the wound. A reverse St. Sebastian. I walk, a strangely shaped sack of white weasels over the shoulder, snowshoes, a pocket of chickenguts, a pocket of piss.

The Dream

1

I rise to my feet in a strange place, again a boy. I am naked beneath a cold kilt of frozen weasels swinging from my waist, black-tipped tails on my thighs, each beast's mouth clenched on a belt of torpid snake, the snake holding his tail in his mouth, cold against my belly. The weasel's eyes looking straight up into mine. Cold. My testicles clutch high, away from the swinging icy shapes.

2

An old Anishinabe comes, in leggings and clout, belly covering breechstring. He is blind, rheum trickling from filmed eyes. A medicine bag hangs from a greased buckskin thong around his throat. He spreads his arms, slowly, and the four winds, green, blue, yellow and red swirl around him as he calls without sound. He holds a withered hand to my mouth and I know I am to spit on it. The hand uncreases, flexes, and grows larger. It finds the medicine bag and pulls out the Mason jar. I am not to speak. The old man opens the jar, rot spills into my nostrils as the shaman falls to the ground, writhing. His flesh begins to split from the crotch and the split moves up his belly and chest. A second body I see within, the old flesh now a husk. He twists, and the dead husk falls away.

3

Stepping lightly from the husk is an old Anishinabe in leggings and clout, belly covering breechstring. The shaman has a purpose and his eyes are bright with it. He gestures, and banishes the red wind, the yellow and the blue. The green wind coils above his head, the uncapped jar appears in his left hand. I am cold beyond shivering, my frozen kilt hangs staring and still. He mimes what I must do.

4

I dip my hands in the jar, lift the contents, and with each weasel at my waist, carefully force the rotting guts into the clenched mouths and up the frozen rectums where sculptured bits of feces remain from the sudden relaxation of death. I watch the marbled eyes unfilm, become a living light. Stiff and mangled bodies ease, fur ripples into place. One by one they drop to the earth, crouch in a circle at my feet, long backs quivering. The snake looses his tail, spirals down my thigh to the ground, coils into the green wind above the shaman's head.

5

The shaman hands me the jar and he does not say but I hear, 'take, eat, for this is your body and blood.' I eat, and drink the juices from the glass. I am naked, warm, my genitals hang. The weasels circle me with urine and the shaman anoints me with that familiar smell, brow, heart, navel. I stand outside my flesh. Weasels run from my mouth, leap balanced to the ground, fold with me into jumbled trunks, the smell of sweet dead wood. My hands drum the echoing earth, netted in roots and tunneled endlessly below. The spiral snake moves in each cell of my flesh, the green wind beats my heart. The shaman chants my eyes to light, spreads his arms. I reach for him.

HEALING THE VOICE

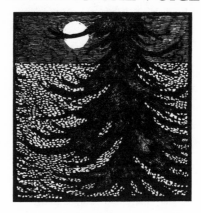

HEALING THE VOICE

1

The forest of winter
night a gasp of white
stars reflecting sharp
snow and blue hands,
needles of black conifers

welcome

the cold eye
opens in the yawn
which empties sound

can the sun be so small
can you so love the white

the glacial surge
of the blue wish inside,

the ending of sound
itself a voice,
here

be silent

2

winter forest light
bones rubbing bark,
rubbing snow,
drifting toward meaning

welcome

the snowwind fills all tracks, all
the vague hieroglyphs which
crook out of white

promises, the end of sound
a snow

healing the dimmed
edges of grousehole, wingtip,
of shadow chafed by milkweed,

the dragging pulse of cold,
the yawn

beneath the silence, the three
surrounds:

the cold pregnancy

the dream snowed in

the wish for white silence,
the return to the moon

3

the quiet of blue bone, the
closed mouth's
gravel:

tongue slowly bites
itself into
a white lace of roots

to filter the throat
and fondle
the half-swallowed stone

to keep the stone

to net the stone
in the cold slow chewing
of unspoken words

to keep the stone from rising

to erode it, roll the stone
in the lace, worry it
smooth

trees have time, glaciers

frost heave:
vomit the stone into light

red is the tongue
mouth open

4

the lolling tongue,
breath white, white wind, the
tracks filling behind

thin into a whine
on swept ice where the bubbles
caught in rising
wait

lick fast
the tongue will not stick

past the muskeg, leatherleaf,
past the deadfall gnarling,
the balsam gathers dark
under boughs, the root
curls into the den

lick
where the belly kisses knees

beneath the foot
trembling in its boot,
beneath snow, buried

deep before hoof,
hair, before
blood heat, below ice

the toad,
backed into dreams
of old thick silences

the closed eye knows
where is light

*where is light
is there sound*

squeezed into the skull
the eye will carry
the dream up,

hand will claw and foot
spade and shove
through frost,

the dream will thaw,
the forgotten voice will
pool and cry spring

fill the lung

6

hand loose,
the fingernail clicks off
a century of weathered
white pine stump

each cold time hard toothed,
each warmth eaten down
below the sawline

is there time

the hollow center
snow mounded

lichens sprinkle orange
rings, leap concentric winters,
nestle in the soft seasons

eat the springwood

under the snowmound,
dry needles, cones, chewed leaves,
old duff nursing moss and

seedling pine, small heaths
wintergreen

trust the center
suckle here

7

edges of spruce
split the moon's rising
and pull her onto boughs

her spending is white,
without wind,
swallowing darkness
in endless clumped flakes

without snow where is thaw

under all this white weight, all
the small crystal tunnels
collapse to april

melting, the wetsong, the entrance,
the beating shared,
the birthbite

again a pulse, still
the thud and surge of vowel
opens the dreaming of tongue

welcome
make noise

THE HERONRY

ALBATROSSES

The girl is alone this summer, more than usual, Dad is working
out of town a lot, and she thinks about him more when he is
gone. She remembers him once, when she was little but really she
supposes not so long ago, telling her about the albatrosses he saw
on Guam when he was stationed there, and how they could soar
and soar on invisible currents of air for days, maybe weeks, he
wasn't sure, and never land. And how the sailors called them
gooney birds because they looked so funny running across the
beach trying to take off. He'd told her also how the fliers thought
that they were dangerous, the gooney birds, how did he say it, 'a
menace to flight,' and his voice had changed by then, and it didn't
make any sense at all to her that a bird who could soar for days or
maybe weeks could be called a menace to flying.

He'd said then that the sailors had to poison them, and when they
were breaking all the eggs they'd called the gooney birds dumb
because they didn't even build proper nests, and when she'd heard
that she'd run away with her hands over her ears hearing 'they had
to honey, men's lives were at stake,' and she had run and run to the
field and sat among the mullein stalks and all the sense she could
make of it with her face in her hands was an engraving in an old
book of Joan of Arc at the stake, the fire just starting, her white
gown trying to billow but bound around with cords.

HER PLACE

After the argument the girl wanders the back forty, scrub pine mixed with popple and just enough raspberry tangles to keep her anger alive. At the far end where the land slopes down to the stream, a stand of cedars work their change, half the trunks upright, the rest leaning in a cacophony of angles or lying collapsed. It is rugged and deeply shadowed, mounds and hollows upholstered ankle deep with sphagnum, light filigreed through cedar fans. As she calms, she fingers stray leaves of last fall's lilies turned by winter into yellowed lace draped limp over moss and heaths. No bright edges anywhere. Here is her place.

A collapse of trunks and moss hummocks makes a canopied chair she thinks of as her throne. She sits. In front of her is her stand of secret ladyslippers, last year's ghosts sprawled where snow flattened them, the new shoots up and green. Two years before she'd transplanted them here with careful hands, then had sat in the throne and commanded them, voice and gesture, to grow, and they had, ample evidence, it seems to her, of her own royal nature — but she is careful to think this only when she is sitting in the throne. It is rarer magic that way, and safer.

Sometimes she takes out the cup she keeps hidden in a hollow and picks her way through moss and trunks to the streambed fifty feet away, fills it and carries it back to drink only when she is properly seated again on the throne, feet crossed at the ankles, which she thinks of as formal. Once last summer, as an experiment, she'd pulled the sphagnum aside until she had a waterseep, then filled the cup with brown bogwater and pretended she was having tea, but a sip ended that. Even alone it was getting harder to pretend.

RITUAL FOR WILDFLOWERS

it is the girl's habit, on her walks
in the woods before things have begun
sprouting much, to invoke spring and
growth with a walking name chant

sing now of wildflowers, sing while you walk:
    star flower, twin flower, winter's green,
    beadlily, sweet fern and sphagnum moss,

sing now arbutus, trailing where you walk,
    bellwort and bedstraw and sweet cicely,
    bloodroot and moccasin, caribou moss,

sing now of groundpine, sing meadow rue,
    wild ginger, maidenhair, pipsissewa,
    gold thread, hepatica, wood anemone,

sing now of shoots, stretching to the day,
sing now of roots, filtering the night,
spring from the earth now, sing yourselves alive.

THE BEGINNING

A long shadow leaps across the moss toward the stream where she glimpses a heron landing, a great blue. Stalker, she picks her way toward him. Hiding in budded alder, she spots him standing just downstream near a pool behind a fallen log. So tall.

When she slides off the bank and finds herself kneedeep and gasping, shoes on, the heron is already in the air and floating around a bend. Shock's inhaled *oh!* still on her face, she follows, wading quietly, the liquid whorls and burbles of spring high water masking any sounds she makes. Stepping over a log: the heron, close. He lowers and leaps from his knees as wings sweep out and gather air and boom down silently. He flies just off the water, staying within the light which falls between the streambank trees and catches hovering flies on its way to the water. When he lands, he looks oddly sideways at her—what she thinks of as *askance.* Then he seems to still himself, not stiffen, just be totally still, and become one with broken-off stumps and leaning branches, nothing moving except the water. Then as she moves, sudden flight.

Downstream they travel, the heron followed by the girl, neither in any hurry. At times she gets close, taking small underwater steps, before he flies. The water runs deeper now, and spreads beyond the banks, so she figures they're getting near the beaver pond and her knees are feeling blue. Tall trees have fallen behind and this low ground is mostly alder and highbush cranberry, with a few tamarack.

She wades around a bend, expecting, but nothing breaks the colors of the stream. Her eye catches him finally, standing on top of a tamarack, just before he lifts off. It astonishes her: she hadn't known that large birds stood on tops of trees with their long legs. Her neck grows goosebumps. But he is flying, and not downstream. His long wings beat and slowly beat away from her toward a distant stand of jackpine on a hillside beyond the flats. As she watches him grow smaller, she flexes her arms like wings, his rhythm.

GREAT BLUE HERON, Ardea herodias

The girl is in town at the library, looking up Heron, great blue. *She takes notes, makes a fact sheet. She wonders how she would look caught in that same list.*

name:
  Great Blue Heron, *Ardea herodias*
  Girl, homo sap

size:
  tip of bill to tailtip . . . . 42" to 52"
  wingspread . . . . 70"
  height   standing . . . . 48"
  height usually . . . . 63"
  height in math class . . . . 32"
  height in dance class . . . . 96"

feather color:
  bluish grey, whiter about head and neck, some black
  dull brown, and straight

beak color:
  bright yellow in young, yellowish in adult
  pink to red, depending on season

PAIRING UP

She sees then other herons flying, first one, then several as her eyes learn how, all headed for the same place although coming from several directions. Lips moving she counts fourteen, fifteen she is sure of, thin double arcs beating then circling down to disappear in the trees. She itches to go there, now, and in a windgust she hears from over there a sound she's never heard. It comes again and shivers with it, this time reminding her of the way the driveway gate creaks and mutters, but this is as if dozens of distant rusty gates are swinging wildly. What are they doing, these solitary birds she's seen all her life, so many of them together?

But she's cold, the sun is late and she has to take care of her little brother—and she's not sure she can navigate through that tangle of low woods. But she'll go soon. No question there.

At suppertime she tells the family of the herons. Dad sits back and smiles and says he'd wondered when she would spot that heronry—it was good timing, he says. When she manages to get out one of the questions crowding her tongue, the one about timing—and before he can answer demands to know why he hasn't shown them to her before, he allows that some things are better found than shown, and by timing, he says, he means that it's best to discover the herons in spring, when they're just pairing up to nest. That way she can watch them through the season, watch the young ones. Maybe learn some things. Then he tells her how to get there dry, down that old logging trail she'd been down for berries, but further in and across the field. He tells her to pick up the trail again next to the three white pines that stand alone on the other side.

Of course, her mother puts in, that doesn't mean she can go off whenever she pleases—after school is out there is her brother to take care of and she'll do well to remember that.

Well, she isn't planning on abandoning her brother or anything else, but she knows there will be no peace if she says it out loud. But she will go to the herons soon, she knows. She knows she has been led.

HERONDANCE

the girl discovers the great blue herons at their nests, and
discovers that to be simultaneously awkward and graceful is ok,
and may have something to do with beauty

standing on the ridge
before the heronry the girl

watches slow beating heron lines
carry her from distance to the nests

her arm drifts from her side

watches spraddle legged leaps
sway great platters of sticks

inside her boot a curling toe

watches lift and wingfall   furl
and open   tilt the windlash   furl

her muscles living shapes beneath the skin

sentinel   she slides an instep up a calf to knee
and throws the leg straight out

now stalks the ridge
strides arching up and toepoint down

assuming beak   she tilts and rolls her head   imagines
weight   and fancies growing breasts and balancing

on stilts she cranes herself around
until her knees bend backward with the birds   finds
her balance for one step   and shouts her way to ground

tossing herons from the trees   each open wing
a harp flung into sky   and sounding in the girl

who rises from her clumsy nest
and scoops the sky up in her wings
to bank and wheel and counterturn—

but startled in her sudden grace   clacks her bill
and balances her flight   with heron croaks

LEG SWINGING SONG

for long walks, as to the heronry
and back, the girl makes up chants,
which she says under her breath
usually, but once in awhile she
hollers them

the berry whose name is straw, is one,
the berry whose name is blue, is two,
    so whatever you do, whatever you chew,
    don't chew on the cherry that chokes.

the berry whose name is bear, is red,
the berry whose name is dew, is too,
    so whatever you do, whatever you chew,
    take care with the cherry that chokes.

the berry whose name is black, is one,
the berry whose name is twin, is two,
    so whatever you chew,
    don't swallow baneberries,
    don't pucker pincherries,
    don't pop elderberries

    and whatever you do
    beware of the cherry that chokes!

BETWEEN THE FACES OF THE LIGHT

closer to the nests this day,
the girl watches landings
high above her in the light,
and finds their shadows seek
her on the forest floor

great paper kites
collapse and collapse into boughs

each landing a falling
each falling a mad fluency

their shadows
careening through pines

fragment down branches
in tatters and flaps

come whole at the ground
then rush forward looming

and as she draws back
wink flat and cut through her unseen

OUT OF THE PALE EGG HUMMING

under the nests for the first time
the girl finds the persistence of
death in the making of life, and
something of what each owes to each

she walks within feathers upright
in nettles like long winged
seeds twirled down from trees

is not aware she kicks apart a wing
of graywhite bones the shade of ragged asters
whose dark stems they fall across

she scans for nests and finds
sown high in spattered branches
light bundles of bone   in wasted feather wrappings

a scaled foot   a sternum   here a yellowed beak
obscure talismen nestled in the bones
like scarabs in the linen of the ibis

in the compass of her eye she spins
from death to hanging death   so many discards   scrap

sees them all compressed   all
drifting like drowned sailors down from sky
to pendulum in shoals of green

shakes away this prettiness to search what's real
picks up a rib   sinew curled around
holds a heartbeat for a moment
in her fingertips

and knows for true the bough breaking nursery rhymes
with nettles singing in her eyes

GREAT BLUE HERON, Ardea herodias

preferred
habitat:

lakes, ponds & swamps, bogs, marshes and
rivers
spring, summer, fall: lakes, ponds & swamps,
bogs, marshes and rivers, woods, fields
winter: my room

migration:

most migrate south in fall; a few solitaries
stay in the north woods for winter, often
dying in storms
none allowed — yet

miscellaneous:

often disheveled looking; feathers preened for
waterproofing; when flying, folds neck and
trails legs; long feathers behind eye suggest
crest
often disheveled looking; when flying, falls when
hears mother's voice

THE PEOPLE OF GLASS

Tell me a story now, like you said.

OK. You'll have to help me start, though, by pretending with me.

How?

Close your eyes. Get down on your hands and knees — yes, really. Make a snowbank in front of you, the tall one next to the driveway. Now make it early spring, one of those first sunny days when you wear your jacket open. Make the snowbank be melting.

Hey.

What.

My knees are getting wet.

Good! Now look where the sun hits the side of the snowbank, where it turns the snow into ice. See how it shines its way into the side of the snowbank a ways, so when you bend way down and look inside, it looks like a lace made of ice, all sparkling in the light? It's like crystal lattice, or like a net made of thin threads of glass. The creatures who live there call it the Worldcrystal, and it's filled with hundreds of rooms and galleries with shiny pillars everywhere.

The creatures who live inside call themselves the people of glass. Now the people of glass think they are very special, and in some ways they are right. The people of glass are hard and clear — they can see right through themselves, and they can see right through each other. Because they are so transparent, they think they do not hide anything from themselves, or from each other. But somewhere in their clarity they hide questions. The people of glass know they are beautiful, and they do sparkle. Everything about them is bright and hard and clear. But the people of glass are cold, and this is a thing they can't explain to themselves.

There is a sadness in the lives of the people of glass, although no one speaks of it. They don't touch each other, or try not to. When they touch each other hard, they chip, so they are cautious. A bigger problem is that sometimes when they touch each other, even softly, they stick together, and can't get loose from each other, so they are afraid to touch for that reason too. And even the bright Worldcrystal they live in is dangerous, for if the glass people don't keep constantly moving, they find themselves stuck to the floor or walls, so they think the smart thing to do is to always keep moving and never stop. There are some stuck ones reaching out to touch them as they constantly walk and walk, who remind them to always keep moving. Bend down again and look way inside — see the sparkling? That's them. They're moving so fast all you can see is the sparkle. So the people of glass keep moving, and they think they know why. But the people of glass don't touch each other, and this too is a thing they can't explain to themselves.

They are afraid to touch and afraid to stop moving, just plain scared, but they call it being sensible, common sense that any fool could understand.

One of the fools who couldn't quite understand was a girl named Winterrain. Unlike most of the glass people, she found herself pulled toward the Great Light at the front of the Worldcrystal. She liked very much to go there, even though when she did, and touched her face, it was wet, like she was weeping, and this confused her, because the people of glass were hard and did not know what weeping was. But even so she found some great pleasure in the Light, some feeling that there was more to life than endlessly walking and walking to keep from getting stuck. After Winterrain had gone to the strongest part of the Light many times, she saw that inside her clear body she had developed a network of fine cracks. This frightened her, but it didn't seem unnatural to her. Most of the people of glass jeered when they saw this, and made fun of her, because she wasn't quite clear anymore. But a few of them found her beautiful, because of the way light would reflect off the cracks and bounce around inside her body. It was like she carried some of the Great Light around inside her now.

To those who found her beautiful, Winterrain confided that she was learning to understand about the people of glass, and she did this quietly, because what she was learning was frightening. But she told those few the truth she was finding out by going to the Light: that they were not the people of glass at all — they were the people of ice. That they were cold and untouching because they were ice. That they were hiding from themselves the fact that they could melt. Now this was scary news. Can you imagine the sparkling and gleaming when they heard? Winterrain also told them that if they touched and joined together, they would live longer and last better in the Light, even though eventually they might still melt away. But by then her friends had become so scared by her words that they ran away, and by then Winterrain was stuck. From then on, everyone who passed her mocked her, poor cracked Winterrain, and called her soft, and other glass people insults — and it was true that she was no longer quite clear, and no longer very hard.

Then, quite suddenly, the Sun hung low on the horizon one day and reached way inside the Worldcrystal, and all the glass people melted in their tracks, even poor cracked Winterrain with light bouncing all around inside her, and as she melted, she understood her name.

What kind of story is that? Everyone dies and it doesn't mean anything!

Wait. I'm not done yet. You see, the people of glass, who were really of ice, when they melted, they all turned into little puddles of water, and the puddles eventually became part of everything in the whole world. Some became part of the birds who came with spring and drank from them, and flew away without their thirst. And some became part of a small pond where the frogs came and sang strange songs all night. Many sank into the earth and found seeds to swell, and those became part of the grasses and wildflowers of the field, and watched the moonlit rabbits dance. And Winterrain, the special one, the one who found out the truth about herself? The puddle of her melting was lifted up into the sky by the Sun, the Great Light, and became part of the air, the air you are breathing as you listen to this tale. So now she is inside you, and touching you, and part of you — and if you are lucky, Winterrain will help you to see what you are.

CRADLES OF STICKS IN HER EYES

under the nests again, she tries to
escape seeing the hanging fallen
nestlings — looking higher, she seeks
visions of a tamer kind of growth,
and is stuck with knowledge instead

throatsounds lift her to
a squall of rusty barks and squawks, lift
her to the interface of leaf and sky

where hungry nestlings wobble open beaks on lumpy necks
and parents' necks curve into question marks
to preen the feathers of the breast
curling tight and neat as spring fern shoots —

jars the image loose as the chicks
croak and yelp at a shadow overhead
in a sudden fish cacophony

echoed thinly as the wind magics out a bone
from the hanging scraps
and rattles it to ground

dropping her eyes:

she tries to keep the ferns, and cannot —
works the shape of question mark —
tries to lick her swollen adam's apple, and cannot

and thinks, *how oddly named*

NESTLING CLOWNS

This day she dances clowns, the squalling windy-feathered chicks
half visible in nests, wearing ruffs of spiky pinfeathers like
elizabethan collars tattered and rumpled, the collars of clowns. She
pulls her shoulders up to make the ruff, holds her fists to clavicles
for stubby penguin-wings and waddles and flaps across the
littered forest floor as if it were her nest. She yawns the mouth
and stretches to imagined fish, overbalancing and staggering.
Making rusty sounds, she pokes and threatens with her beak, and
walking charlie chaplin finds a deer scrape where this morning a
buck too saw the nestlings, she thinks, and scuffed and dug his
laughscrape out ten feet, so the girl narrows her feet to hooves,
leaps and scuffs her running shoes, adds her own grit to the scrape
and laughs, runs leaping and tossing her horns till halfway home.

TRACKING

Mostly it was Dad who taught her that to track and stalk, you had to become. Had to wear the other creature's skin whether feathered or furred. He showed her once, shyly, how he crouched to deer-height and moved down the trail—without leafslaps—and she saw all kinds of sign she wouldn't have seen walking human: the tuft of hair in bark where a doe scratched her back, the scarred sapling where a yearling buck rubbed velvet, there the long exuberant hoofscrape tossing sand. He taught her ways of knowing otherness. She learned to read where red squirrels gnawed their cones, and how close she could get to a marsh hawk's nest before she'd get screamed at. How to read a rabbit nibbled sapling back through time to know the height of winter snow, how to know fox den from badger by shape and smell, how to make mousesqueaks to bring bobcat kittens close. She discovered how to create a stillness within herself unbroken by mosquito slaps. And she learned on her own some private ways of knowing otherness.

GREAT BLUE HERON, Ardea herodias

eye color:
golden
brown (hazel?)

voice:
low hoarse croak (warning), squawks, guttural clacking, also screeches, barks, gabbling, chopping sounds
rarely sweet; often hoarse croaks, high shrieks, yells, groans, babble, laughter, sobs

leg/foot color:
black
pink to black, depending on season

food:
mainly fish and frogs, also toads, salamanders, snakes, lizards, mice, voles, chipmunks
grass seeds, bird eggs, cow milk, roots, flesh of large mammals, fish, school lunch

RITUAL FOR HERONBEING

She stands in the clearing and stamps and stamps one bare foot, hands above her hair, her knotted forehead smoothing with each stamp, loosing the human, letting her face go slack. She does not know her ritual is old as any dance upon the drumskin earth. She shrugs off her shirt and jeans, kicking them away without breaking the oneleg stamp. Moulting. Shedding the skin. The pulsing of her foot upon the heart of earth until the rhythms match. She knows she cannot fill with heron until she is empty and pure: without voice, without thought or thumb, without time. Only this stamping. Behind her eye she carries an image of transparent fish eggs sinking through clear water, and follows them down.

Some days she can't do it, but today is good. She carries the rhythm inside and keeps it while her outside makes a stillness. Arms grown to her sides, her body ripples as if fishswimming in place, makes the movement larger as she feels the wings emerging from her shoulderblades. Her hands lift and sculpt her skull into the beak, shaping it longer, longer. Now she is.

NEST TREE IN THE WHEEL OF LIGHT

in which the girl wakes in storm, fears for the
nestlings in the heronry, so seeks within the
nest tree a resolution of her fears, and finds in
time not exactly safety, but a longer view

lightning shot   upright in bed
goosebumps wind her toes into the rug
stands she now   gathering

the nests are in the storm

steeples fingers at her breast   lifts them high
wrists together   lets the hands
drop open   seedcase splitting from the seed

thunder narrows her

lets arms fall   stiffen
to the angle of the jackpine branch

window curtains whipping in her ears

she welcomes boughs   welcomes
bark glissading up her roots and limbs
carries needles to the edge of self and storm

calls up nest   weaves the old stick circle
knows its sag and bounce   to parents landing
taking flight   tenses muscles into nestlings' growth

a chill pebbles her with
thunderclap and rain   a glare   and she is

nest and tree and black in lightning's doubled night
of storm and bending   windcaught
a weight in her goes light   catches
on a branch below   a small flapping white

curtains in the black square of rain

watches time sprinkle bones from her
feels the moss she's tangled in reach up
to gather them   a greening of her roots
hears the jaws of small mothers gnawing calcium
to set their milks against the hunger in the den

heavy on her arms the great circle of the nest
heavy in her trunk new rings of growth

more lightly at her bud breast
the circle of the nipple and the mother's tooth
fish bone   to feathered bone   to furred

she sets the circles down and joins the bed

stillness   gathering

ON THE DAY OF WIND

The sentinel herons ride thin treetops which pitch and roll ten feet from side to side, wings held crook'd and knees sharply backbent, long toes curled around pinebark like huge redwings clinging to fifty foot cattails. One rides a tree for a time, then uncurls his toes and without moving wings sails to a treetop twenty feet away, toe-hooking a branch — then again, again, island hopping.

Today nothing has its neck pulled in, today everyone flies without working: the windknocked raven banking from a kamikaze blackbird, the high fishstealing eagle circling. Herons whip by like great tornloose sails, turn and hang still for improbable moments.

Gusts toss the rookery clatter in and out of the girl's ears. A fleet of tall cumulus sails in blue distance beyond the rafted nests tossing in the clear. Returning herons board the nests like pirates boarding galleons, gripping the gunwales and flapping, croaking while the passengers jabber back, swaying precariously as their swords dive deep into the confusion of yellow beaks.

Fifty feet below, tethered to the seafloor, the girl rides her tiptoes.

GIRL

This girl you're always telling stories about — what's her name?
I'm not going to tell you.
Why not?
Because she never thought her name fit her, and she was afraid of it. Sometimes names fit people, you know, but mostly they don't. You hear people say that the name matches the person, and act surprised, like it was some sort of marvelous coincidence. But what they don't know is that some names grow over people, and take them over like mould on a loaf of bread. The girl knew she had a special kind of name, called a Prime Name, that had this power of changing people to fit it, so she was scared of it.
Come on.
Really. Names like "Gertrude" or "Nancy" or "Muffy"—it's Names like that you have to watch out for. "Birch" and "Victor" and "Seymour" are Prime Names that can turn you really weird. And "Ethel" and "Harold" can have awful effects on your life.

Anyway, these Prime Names have the power to turn people into their Namesakes, sort of. Animals and birds all have Prime Names, too, but for each kind of creature there's only one Prime Name, which is why all black bears look alike, and all herons and sparrow hawks. Their Prime Names aren't what we call them, though — all the creatures' Prime Names are unknown to people, and the creatures want it that way. But people tell everyone their names.

With children, Prime Names change the way their faces look, and the way they walk and stand, and probably the way they might jump a mud puddle. Some Names can't jump mud puddles. The girl knew she had a Prime Name, but she also knew that if she didn't feed it, it would lose its power. You feed a Name by using it, of course. But the Tenant of the Name is the only really important user. If the Tenant says it out loud, or even thinks it, the Name gets more powerful. But if she doesn't use it, or think it, the Name goes hungry and shrinks up and hibernates. That's not so easy, not even thinking your Name. The girl didn't use the Name at all, unless absolutely forced to, like for teachers the first day of school. She was scared to use it, and she was smart.

She started refusing the Name when she was still in her crib—she screamed whenever she heard it, so she had the family trained in three weeks. So when she was little, she learned to think of herself as just 'girl,' in small letters. But later on, when she was seven or eight, she thought of herself as 'GIRL,' capitalized. She learned this from Saturday morning Tarzan movies with BOY, whose name she envied until a few years later when she realized how boys were. But she kept the style anyway. Later on, even after she learned about boys, she developed a secret True Romance belief: that a boy could cure a Prime Name. Looking right into the girl's eyes, and being absolutely honest, he had to say the Prime Name and the words "I Love You!" and the Name would lose all its power. She always thought that BOY would be the boy's name when it happened to her. But he wouldn't look like Tarzan's Boy.

Nobody ever thought to call the girl by her middle name. No one ever gave her a nickname, either. Sometimes she wanted to be called Wintergreen or Sandpiper or some name like that, but it never happened. She figured that someone else had to do the naming, and no one ever did. Sometimes she hinted a little, but it didn't help. Her dad called her Princess, but that never felt like a name to her. Eventually, nobody called her by her true Name either, because she would hit them. The only worry she had about any of this, now and then, was when she thought about what she would be called when she was thirty.

So what did they call her? They must have called her something!

Nothing. She never got called by any name. People learned to just walk up to her and start talking. She'd ignore them if they didn't. Sometimes they started by saying words like "Say," or "Hey." So anyway, that's all there is to why the girl doesn't get called by her Name.

Is my name a Prime Name?

I'm not going to tell you.

Is yours?

I'm not going to tell you.

Aren't you even going to tell me the girl's Name? You have to!

Nope.

GREAT BLUE HERON, *Ardea herodias*

nesting: in colonies, from a few nests to two or three
                hundred; usually in trees; large nest platforms
                of sticks lined with plant stalks, grasses,
                feathers; sites used for generations; pairs
                change year to year; heronries may be several
                miles from fishing areas; nesting herons fly to
                fish in all directions from the nest
                data unavailable; subject is not mature; doubtful
                nesting will take place at all, based on
                experiences with small brother

eggs: three to six, greenish-blue, smooth to slightly
                rough; laid in Minnesota April 25–May 20;
                incubation 25–29 days; two or three survive
                to fledging
                hundreds, subject is told; color unknown

mating: males dance to the females, they dance back;
                males also dance combat with other males
                data unavailable, subject is not mature;
                practice available at dances after football,
                basketball games, beaches, drive-ins

THE RAGE RESERVED FOR LOVE

*in which the girl discovers an almost fullfledged
heron who has fallen from the nest before he was
able to fly. She is enchanted, tries to join with
him somehow, but comes to know she cannot save him
from the coming night*

1   *Bird in the Bushes, From the Treetops*

the spear head rises from green hazelbrush
unfolding from dark plumage,
rises more, like some unguessed serpent
lifting from the sea   a golden eye

the lump inside her thaws   she
swallows the high note in her throat
a tense step forward   two

the grounded fledgling lifts a foot
rocks back   plants it   again
gauges her   keeps the stump between

slowly they circle in the top of her brain
where the grey prince has fallen from the sky to her
while the belly of her brain sings fear   sings

stop.   neck looped   he bows low   rapidly bobs

from the waist she mirrors him
makes a leg and mantles it with wing
stretches up   chin high

tall they are in the top of her brain
stately they will be
she arches her feet in a long slow strut

he backs around the stump again   each
foot held   static in light   then
set down   the rhythm of a stagger   slowed

she catches in a wind the musty smell of him
of nest   slowly they stalk while
the belly of her brain sings fear   sings

stop.   he swells   feathers all erect
doubles his beak on his neck   held flat
held aimed   hangs wings open from the elbows

he is hers!   she rushes him   her prince in gray
throws around him her hands   his darting spear
tries to furl buffeting wings   is struck   his musk
his feathers live on spines   jumps back

a feint   a lunge on backbent legs

the girl   the bird   half crouched
for a lover ready   for an enemy

sees him falter   shiver
pluck a broken feather on his wing

sings stop now   stop

2   *We are Children Here*

she sucks a forearm welt and loses balance   sits
on every grace she found upon the ridge

knows not what to grasp

looks at her hands to find
pinfeathers floating in her palms   and clenches them

she would embrace this musky flesh
and hurl him from the floor of this green sea
to be the harp inside her dance or

take him   where?

the heron lifts his drowning lance to blue
doubles it back and beats his wings
and thrusts with all himself to air   rises
for a beat   and shivers down unstrung

a hunger here which cannot fly
she cannot balance this

lets him stalk about   beak up and wide
as if the sky in all this capsized nestless world
might rain a frog

3   *Owning Up*

what act?   climb a nest like him to fall?   she
closes her eyes   in full extension stands
throws wide her wings   and feels her fledgling

lift from the nest on a gust-caught billowed wing
and topple onto flailing air

sprawl down branches and blur to ferns and stand
jarred   spreadwinged and muttering

she sees this and cannot   she knows too much now
no mother   no father
now not in the nest   never was

soft croaking throat   filled with rust and time
and empty of fish
by the down in her fists   she knows too much now

THE DANCE OF BITTER HERBS

she has run through trees until she can't, and
her face welted from branches, she sucks air

sourdock and nettles!   bloodroot!
she wants to rip them out of earth
and stuff her mouth   suck their bitters

she wants the dry keen of grasshoppers
to be the witness of her ears

her skin is lumpy as her adam's apple
and she works to accept that eggs demand deaths

she knows it all connects
all   but this is wrong

every feather   every leaf
should tremble in the presence of her grief
but they will not

and the herons sitting sentinel ignore the fledgling—
he is not

> *she grips the sharp edge of her egg*
> *watching blood flow from her palms*
> *chooses hard   and leaps*
> *into the ancient circle   she is alive*
> *and he is not*
>
> *there are no cradles rocking anywhere*
> *all hanging   balanced   all stilled*

beginnings are endless
endings are bitterly brief

the girl begins to sense
that she is a beginning
who thinks she is an end
that she is a beginning
who has no end

caught like every pulsing throat
in the great revolving
circle of the nipple and the mother's tooth

STILL LIFE FOR INK AND BRUSH

soon they'll leave, she knows, and
from the ridge looks back at their
ancient tableau

all facing west
all around her   becalmed

herons burning out fleas

stiff legg'd on branches
halfway up trunks

herons bathe in reddening light

sitting nests   balanced
on the whitewashed crests of pines

the heronry basks

wings flopp'd and elbows crook'd
and beaks cocked to the sun

huge unkempt origami birds
scattered grey on green

WILD CANARIES

Up to the high pasture this morning, in the August buzz of grasses gone to seedheads hanging over sorrel reddening, only the tallest toughest flowers open now, even the thousand thistles turned now from cobalt to white, and she expects when she reaches the crest a sea of thistle white sprinkled with tobacco stalks of dock and mullein spears still blooming yellow at their tips. As she hikes uphill each step creates a dusty surge of grasshoppers, green ones leaping, the grey kind unfolding black and yellow wings, hard to see until, all clicking as they move, and above them dragonflies with tails of red and powder blue and green, and it is August, but it feels to her like beginnings.

At the crest where she thinks *Now white, a sea of white,* at the crest a froth of gold, goldfinches every-which-angled on the thistles, and in the sunlight like gauze is thistledown floating everywhere, and finches ride the seedheads, singly dancing across the field like the small chop and dither of water on top of the flock's deeply swelling wave which advances on her as she stands amazed. First a white puffed thistlehead, then a sudden bent and golden bloom which pulls each bit of fluff from its seed and tosses what is left onto the breeze as children do the milkweed pods, then off to light on another, all these goldfinches dip and lift and fall, and as they rise each sings. All around her now the flock, parting an arm's length on either side, and she thinks of schooling minnows in the shallows parting for her ankles. The flock moves slowly through her as a sun-chopped wave, slowly, one that's come all distances and more and unready yet to break. *Oh their slow surrounding swell*—she names it *Thistle speed,* and *This day, this day,* she says, *is gold,* and in the breeze the thistles rise and dip, and her knees dip and rise, and the finches lift and fall and lift, and as they rise they sing.

It feels to the girl like beginnings, or is it something endless, something of great circles and of waves, swelling gentle waves circling time for century after century but always new, renewed, and she is in it, of it, adrift on this golden day of finches and of thistledown, wondering still as her knees dip and rise how something endless can feel so like beginnings.

WHERE AM I?

You ready to tell this story yet?

Maybe. The only way I can find out is by telling it. Are you ready to listen?

I've been ready for half an hour.

So crawl under the covers. Okay, here it is. Once there was a girl who was lost. Oh, she knew where she was, all right, or where she was told she was, but she was still lost. Her problem was, she was losing herself. The girl used to know where she was—she hadn't always been lost. As a matter of fact, she never thought about whether she was lost or not, because when you're not lost, you don't think about it. But now she did.

I can't see anything—where are we?

Good question, but hard to answer. She used to be in a brighter place than she is now. But it was a smaller place than now. It was as if she'd been outdoors all her life, and now she was inside. But outdoors, in the forests and fields and the brightness, she never had to think much, or decide much—she could just *be*. Now she's inside, inside a house whose walls are her own skin. From the outside, the house seemed smaller than the forest and fields, but once she got inside, she found endless rooms and cellars and attics, many with open doors and many more with doors locked. There were broad open halls and narrow passages with low ceilings that pressed down on her. There were ballrooms and kitchens and bedrooms and parlors, and a whole lot of closets. There were musty rooms that needed airing and a few rooms with windows open wide. Some of the rooms were bright with laughter and the sparkling of the good kind of tears, and some rooms were warm and orange from fireplaces, and some, lower down, were chilly and filled only with darkness, and some below those were icy and filled with huge coiling serpent shapes that never stopped moving.

She didn't know how she got into the house inside her skin, and she didn't know how to get out of it and back to the forest, but one thing she was sure of: she was lost.

There were sometimes other presences in the house with her—not spooky scary ones, really, but stubborn ones that had no ears, that couldn't seem to hear her. The presences were loud voices, mostly. Once, when she was standing in a cool room filled with old lace and faded photos and such, and feeling especially lost, this enormous man's voice said in a false-hearty way, *"NONSENSE, YOU'RE NOT LOST, YOU'RE RIGHT HERE!"* It made her very angry very fast. She knew what lost was. It made her scared, too, because the voice could know what she was feeling, even though it wouldn't listen to her words.

Another time, when she was sitting in a child's nursery absently piling up letter blocks and spelling out L-O-S-T, a woman's voice boomed into her and said, *"SILLY, YOU'RE HOME, NOT LOST. I SWEAR, THAT CHILD . . ."* and then it faded out. That time her heart speeded up and wouldn't slow down for a long time, even after she shouted back at the voice a while later. She couldn't remember after what she had shouted, though, and didn't really want to.

One room she went into was a room where, if she let her hands relax at her sides, she could feel another hand take hers, and hold it gently — and somehow it wasn't scary. She went back sometimes. There was another room like that, only it was shoulder patting instead of hand holding, and she felt little there and didn't go back. There were no voices in these rooms, and after the first times, no surprises.

Why did you stop?

Well, I'm not sure what happens next, and it's late now — I know, it's my fault, we started late. But here's a bargain: I'll tell you the rest tomorrow night, if you'll go to sleep now.

But I want to know what happens.

So do I, okay? But so far, I don't. Deal?

THE WHITE DREAM

In her dream are two figures, a white eagle and a man. And herself, a girl hanging back or just a watching thought. They are in a boundless white space, all featureless and white except for a green oak and the scarlet clothing of the man.

The white eagle is soaring and swooping incredibly, testing the limits of flight, now straining so high it is lost, now dropping, expanding with a rush of black talons. But the man is its master, he has trained it, and the white eagle flies on the tether of his eyes. The man watches the performance, commands rolls, circles left, circles right with theatrical gestures of the hand. The white eagle whirls and spins in the air like an ice skater. The girl's lips do not move but she hears her voice demand, *Why would an eagle do that for you?* The man glances at her, as if he had known she were watching, turns his eyes back to the spinning eagle and replies, *For promises.*

When the dream dissolves it sticks with her, uncomfortably. She does not know what it means. She finds herself replaying it.

THE GREY PRINCE

I know what happens now.

Finally.

Watch it. Now the girl is in the house, remember, and it seems like she has been wandering the house inside her skin for a long time. Then it changes.

She is walking across a ballroom floor, and the floor is made of pale egg-shells, complete large eggs that she knows are empty. The ballroom walls are made of mirrors, and she can see a thousand of herself stepping gingerly across the fragile eggs, trying to make herself light. She knows somehow that if the eggs break she will fall right through the floor, and the mirrors will show no image. Then, right out of nowhere, the man's voice booms, *"I WISH SHE'D SNAP OUT OF IT,"* and the mirrors all change to funhouse mirrors, and her thousand images all shrink or get fat or turn into stick girls with long feet, and all the eggs shatter. As she falls through the floor in slow motion, she sees small dead chicks in among the broken shells, and small dead girls in sunsuits, and both the chicks and girls are withered and dusty, with curled up legs, and can't have taken up much space in the large eggs.

Now she is falling slowly, through thick air, and her stomach is still above her somewhere, and when she looks up she sees pieces of eggshell following her down, and is horrified to think that some of the mummified chicks or girls might float down after her. She looks down, just as a pair of enormous grey wings appears, and a heron's folded neck, and she can see one eye cocked upward as if measuring her fall, and the next second — oof! — she lands on the heron's back and those huge wings carry her away from the house, and the girl is very busy holding on — but she isn't lost.

She looks at the heron she's riding, and hastily adjusts her grip so she won't ruffle his feathers any more than she has to. He is beautiful and grey with hints of blue, and she sits just behind his great head, which is pulled back close to his wings, with his neck looping under it. She isn't especially scared, which surprises her — she feels like someone is holding her close. He wears his crest feathers like a crown, and she decides to name him her grey prince. They are flying over the forest and the fields, and she is so glad to be out of that house inside her skin. She is so glad to be back *here* again, where those voices don't intrude, where everything is simple and clear.

But the moment she thinks that, the heron swoops down to land on the shallow edge of a small lake, in a reedbed. She slides down his back and gets shakily to her feet. He looks at her askance, and she knows she is to watch, only watch. He stalks out into the reeds, then stops, standing poised in the shallows. The water is a mirror, and the reed reflections bend away. He waits, then, and she waits. Of a sudden too fast to see, his head spears the water and comes up with a frog in the end of his beak. He tosses his beak into the air, flips the frog loose, snaps once and the frog disappears. Her arms tremble. And she thinks of the frog's fingers outlined for an instant against the sun before the beak clacked, thinks of the tiny egg girls' hands.

The heron walks back to her and stares sidelong, as if wanting some reaction. She works at thinking of him as her prince. Does he see her trembling? Is she feeling lost?

He swings his beak, she climbs back on, and soon they are above the trees again. They are circling the heronry, and as they circle, time circles with them. She sees the herons arriving in the spring, catches glimpses of the courtship dances through the trees. She sees nests being repaired, and fresh grasses woven for the final layer. Circles again and sees the eggs laid, five in that nest, three over there. The grey prince circles through the hatching time — but some eggs don't hatch, just wobble a few times, then go quiet, and by the next circle those have disappeared from the nests, and the remaining chicks are all in clown costume, and the parents are not in mourning.

The grey prince flies her away then, to another small lake, where an old heron with patchy feathers walks the shore, looking shrunken and hungry, and she sees that there is something wrong with his eyes. But she also sees how he holds his head up as he waits to die. The shore where he walks bursts with life, swallows darting and swooping low after bugs, fish lazing through the spatterdock leaves which strain toward the light. High above, an osprey soaring, below, cattails and arrowheads aimed at the sun, while underwater, through their stems, a school of baby bullheads wriggles, shepherded by the mother. The old one drops a feather on the sand, part of this.

The grey prince motions her onto his back again, and again they fly. This time they spiral high, high next to the great cumulus clouds, and the towering thunderheads have such fierce beauty that she gets scared. She yells at him then, she accuses him and life of being unfair. She yells demands at his silent skull until he turns it halfway up, looking at her with one gleaming eye. The eye seems to spin, and makes her dizzy, so she holds on tighter. But in the spinning eye she sees herself a ways back, in a sunsuit, chasing after a swallowtail butterfly. Then as she falls further into his eye, she sees herself again, older now, wearing jeans, watching that same butterfly — but now seeing at the same time the caterpillar that went to make it, the tattered leaves it fed on, the helpless dangling of the chrysalis, the wings growing tattered like the leaves as their colors begin to fade, the last trembling of the wings as the swallowtail returns to the earth. All this she sees spiraling in the grey prince's eye, and she is very quiet.

The heron never speaks, he gives nothing away, but he keeps beating his wings, and suddenly they arrive in the ballroom again. The room is huge, and very different. This time the floor is of old polished wood, gleaming like the prince's eye in the light from the crystal chandeliers. All the mirrors are back on the wall. As she slides off his back, old fashioned violin music begins. He draws himself up, facing her, opens his wings, and bows. She finds herself making a curtsy in return. He offers his wingtip, courtly, and she takes it with grace. And although she doesn't know how, she is dancing a minuet with the great blue heron prince, stately as anything, and calm.

What's the opposite of lost? That's how she feels right now. But still, she keeps noticing the fingers of her hand as they touch the tips of his feathers. They circle and they dip and bow, to the old music lightly heard and lightly danced. And as they move, she sees in the mirrors lining the walls that she is dancing with an elegant young man in a pearl grey suit. Their hands touch only on the fingertips, and he is looking into her eyes. But the girl knows there will be no waltz here — a minuet is as close as they can be. And just as well.

Hey. Are you asleep?

OCTOBER SOUNDS, FOR ULNA FLUTE, GOSHORN AND COCHLEA

she walks the empty heronry
seeking the shapes of balance,
and finds a kind of harmony in
this lovely season of dying back

she scuffs mute through boneyards
signed with droppings streaked on bark
and uprooted jackpine snags   charred and white
and jagged in the duff like antlers painted for a ritual

mingled with a few clumps of breast down
and the long hollow bones of the last nesting's fallen

scattered now   propped in dry bracken
such tendon-carved grace   hollowed
for flight   borne but once   in the falling
when the wind inside the honeycomb splintered into air

now gusting south   with a horn bell of geese
garbling a brass   haunt   haunt
the goshorn echoed in the flutes
whose chambers are sucked into sound in the northern wind

echoed in the cochlea coiled inside the ear inside
the girl   who lifts one bone
and blows across the open end
and fingers its length blinking   faces

south   grasps it by the sculpted joint
and rips the long bone across and across the wind

John Caddy lives in Minneapolis with his wife, three cats and his garden. He spends his time writing, teaching writing, woodworking, and practicing writing therapy. A native of the Mesabi Range in northeastern Minnesota, he grew up knowing he was part of the pine forest which surrounded him.

He has taught high school English, taught at the University of Minnesota for eight years, was a founder of the Poets-in-the-Schools program, and has been writer-in-residence in over two hundred schools. For several years, he taught environmental studies in the north woods near Lake Itasca.

His poems have been published in many journals and anthologized. He has also written for public radio. In 1984, 'The Heronry' was staged in collaborative performance fusing dance, music and poetry.

A special request: Caddy believes the sounds and rhythms of poetry to be as important as the words, and invites the reader to say his poems out loud.